WORLD'S FASTEST AIRCRAFT

APEX

By Brienna Rossiter

WWW.APEXEDITIONS.COM

Apex is distributed by North Star Editions:
sales@northstareditions.com | 888-417-0195

Produced for Apex by Red Line Editorial.

Photographs ©: Jim Ross/NASA, cover, 1; Shutterstock Images, 4–5, 6–7, 9, 14, 15, 18–19, 26–27; Jim Ross/NASA/DVIDS, 8, 24; NASA/DVIDS, 10–11, 22–23; NASA/Bell Aircraft Company/DVIDS, 12–13; Staff Sgt. Keith James/US Air Force/DVIDS, 13, 29; NASA, 16–17, 20–21; DARPA/DVIDS, 25

Library of Congress Control Number: 2021918400

ISBN
978-1-63738-168-7 (hardcover)
978-1-63738-204-2 (paperback)
978-1-63738-272-1 (ebook pdf)
978-1-63738-240-0 (hosted ebook)

Printed in the United States of America
Mankato, MN
012022

NOTE TO PARENTS AND EDUCATORS

Apex books are designed to build literacy skills in striving readers. Exciting, high-interest content attracts and holds readers' attention. The text is carefully leveled to allow students to achieve success quickly. Additional features, such as bolded glossary words for difficult terms, help build comprehension.

TABLE OF CONTENTS

CHAPTER 1

SPEEDY SPY PLANE

An SR-71 soars above the clouds. The spy plane is on a mission. Its sleek, pointed body sneaks past enemy **radar**.

The SR-71 flies 80,000 feet (24,000 m) off the ground. This is right at the edge of space.

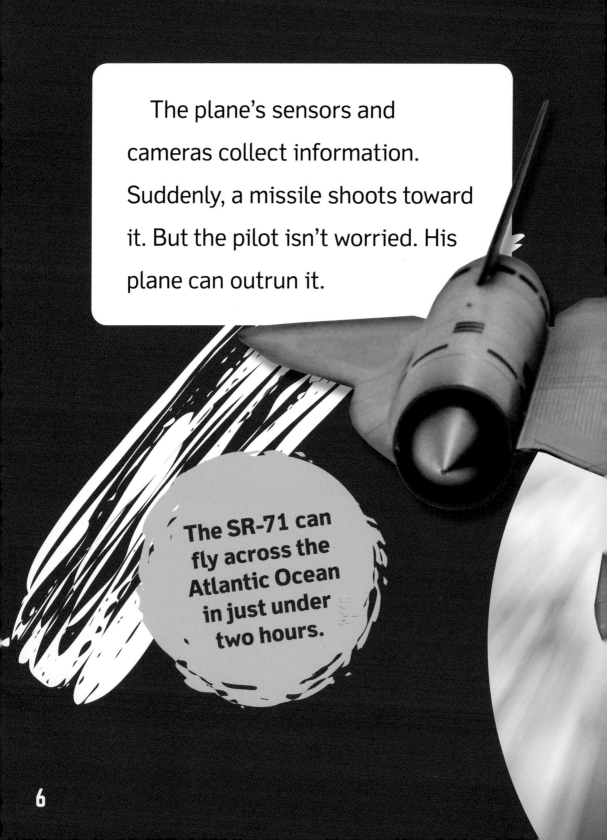

The plane's sensors and cameras collect information. Suddenly, a missile shoots toward it. But the pilot isn't worried. His plane can outrun it.

The SR-71 can fly across the Atlantic Ocean in just under two hours.

As the plane races away, it gets very hot. But the pilot's suit protects him. He flies safely home.

As the SR-71 flies, the outside of its body can reach 600°F (316°C).

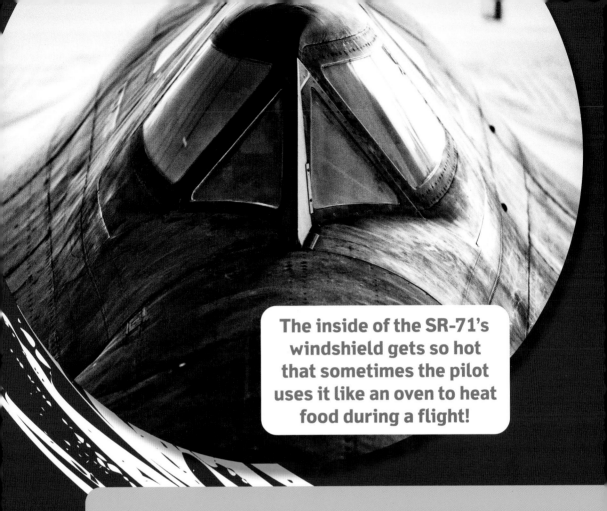

The inside of the SR-71's windshield gets so hot that sometimes the pilot uses it like an oven to heat food during a flight!

AMAZING ENGINES

The SR-71 flies so fast it needs special engines. The engines slow down the air that hits them. They also burn special fuel. The plane's heat would make regular fuel explode.

CHAPTER 2

INCREASING SPEED

To fly fast, planes need lots of power. Many use **jet engines**. Jets were invented in the 1940s. Some flew faster than the speed of sound. The Bell X-1 did this first.

The Bell X-1 first flew faster than sound in 1947. Later, this plane flew more than twice the speed of sound.

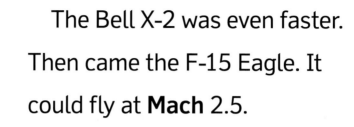

The Bell X-2 was even faster. Then came the F-15 Eagle. It could fly at **Mach** 2.5.

The Bell X-2 Starbuster's wings were swept back so air wouldn't slow the plane down as much. It reached Mach 3.196 in 1956.

The US military flew its first F-15 Eagle in 1972.

SONIC BOOMS

As planes fly, they **displace** air. At Mach 1 or faster, they cause sonic booms. These sounds can be very loud. They can even damage buildings!

Countries made more powerful planes. The MiG-25 could fly at Mach 3.2. The MiG-31 wasn't as fast. But it could fly higher and longer.

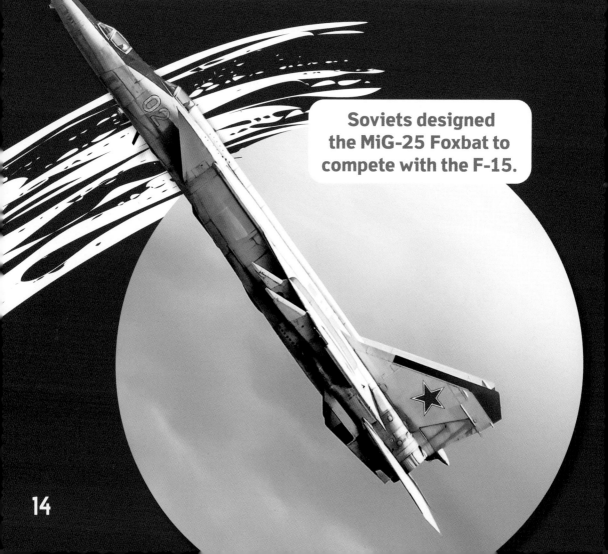

Soviets designed the MiG-25 Foxbat to compete with the F-15.

The MiG-31's top speed was Mach 2.83.

The MiG-25 and MiG-31 are still two of the world's fastest planes.

CHAPTER 3

FASTEST JETS

The SR-71 was made in the 1960s. But it's still the fastest jet plane. The SR-71 was based on the Lockheed A-12. Both planes flew faster than Mach 3.

The SR-71 is the fastest plane not powered by rockets.

The A-12 was a top-secret stealth plane used by the CIA.

At that speed, heat from **friction** can melt some metals. So, the A-12 was made of titanium. This metal can stand high heat.

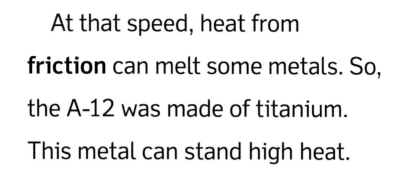

PASSENGER PLANES

Some passenger planes have flown faster than sound. The Concorde could reach Mach 2. It flew from 1976 to 2003. Then high costs ended its flights.

The SR-71 used a titanium **alloy**. And it was painted black. The paint helped cool the plane.

Black paint can help a plane hide from radar.

No SR-71 was ever shot down by enemy planes.

The SR-71 was nicknamed the Blackbird because of its dark paint.

CHAPTER 4

OTHER RECORDS

The fastest **manned** airplane is the X-15. It reached Mach 6.7 in 1967. A bomber carried it into the air. Then it used rockets to fly and steer.

To save fuel, the X-15 rode into the air under the wing of a B-52 bomber.

Some **unmanned** aircraft go even faster. NASA's X-43A is the fastest jet. It traveled Mach 9.6 in 2004. In 2010, the Falcon HTV-2 reached Mach 20. It used rockets.

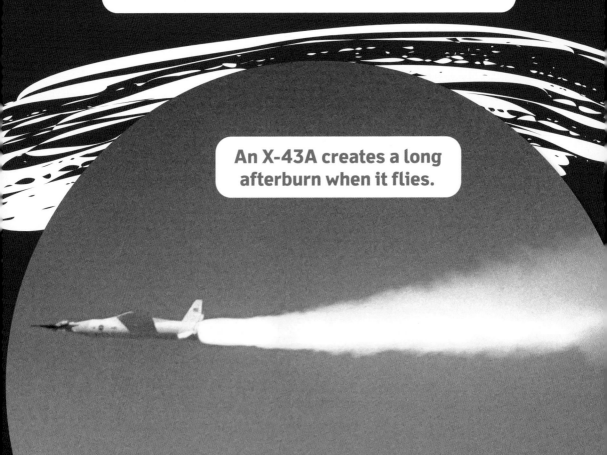

An X-43A creates a long afterburn when it flies.

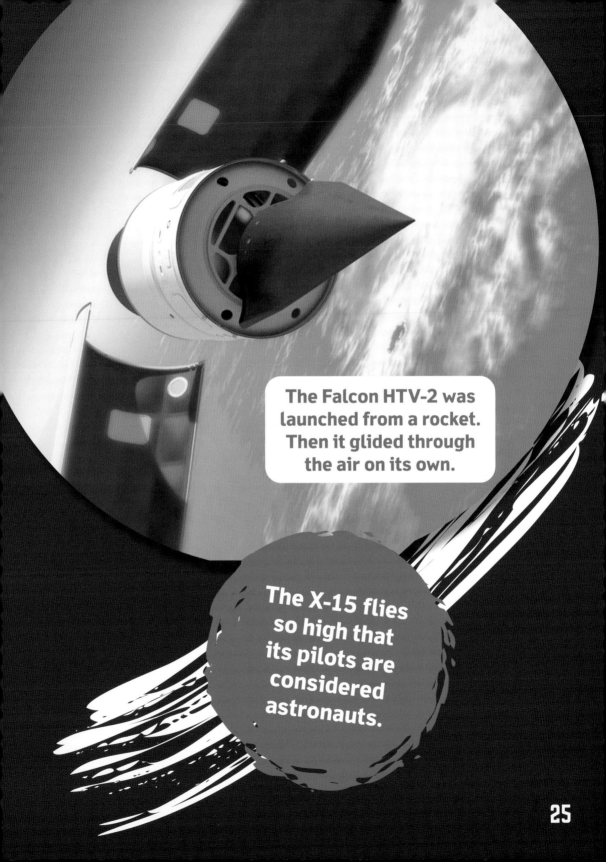

The Falcon HTV-2 was launched from a rocket. Then it glided through the air on its own.

The X-15 flies so high that its pilots are considered astronauts.

New planes may reach higher speeds. But planes take years to develop. For example, in 2021, work on the SR-72 entered its eighth year.

People often create models or illustrations as they design a new plane.

QUIET DESIGNS

Many countries have laws against **supersonic** flights over land. But scientists are testing new designs. These planes would displace less air. So, they would be quieter.

COMPREHENSION QUESTIONS

Write your answers on a separate piece of paper.

1. Write a sentence describing the main ideas of Chapter 2.

2. Would you want to fly in a supersonic plane? Why or why not?

3. What is the fastest jet plane?

> **A.** the X-1
> **B.** the SR-71
> **C.** the MiG-31

4. Why might countries make laws against supersonic flights?

> **A.** People don't want to go places quickly.
> **B.** People don't want noise and damage from sonic booms.
> **C.** People don't want planes to save fuel.

5. What does **protects** mean in this book?

*But the pilot's suit **protects** him. He flies safely home.*

   A. keeps safe
   B. creates danger
   C. causes sadness

6. What does **develop** mean in this book?

*But planes take years to **develop**. For example, in 2021, work on the SR-72 entered its eighth year.*

   A. to take pictures
   B. to stop trying
   C. to plan how to make

Answer key on page 32.

GLOSSARY

alloy
A metal made by mixing metals or other materials together.

displace
To push something out of the way.

friction
A force that happens when objects rub against one another, often slowing them down.

jet engines
Engines that create power by burning fuel mixed with air.

Mach
A unit for measuring speed. Mach 1 is the speed of sound. Mach 2 is twice the speed of sound. The speed of sound changes with air conditions. But it is often more than 760 miles per hour (1,220 km/h).

manned
Carrying a pilot, passengers, or crew.

radar
A system that sends out radio waves to locate objects.

supersonic
Faster than the speed of sound.

unmanned
Not carrying any people, not even a pilot.

TO LEARN MORE

BOOKS

Hamilton, S. L. *The World's Fastest Planes*. Minneapolis: Abdo Publishing, 2021.

Howard, Sherry. *Top Ten Fastest Planes*. Vero Beach, FL: Rourke Educational Media, 2020.

Lanier, Wendy Hinote. *Fighter Jets*. Lake Elmo, MN: Focus Readers, 2019.

ONLINE RESOURCES

Visit **www.apexeditions.com** to find links and resources related to this title.

ABOUT THE AUTHOR

Brienna Rossiter is a writer and editor who lives in Minnesota. She enjoys reading about animals and science.

INDEX

Answer Key:
1. Answers will vary; 2. Answers will vary; 3. B; 4. B; 5. A; 6. C